Web Leslie

NOW & THEN

*"ponderings in a
pool of poems"*

3/24/13

Alex & Linda
Enjoyed the Chance to.
witness great golf with
you two and thanks for
the lunch.
You might enjoy these
poems as many about Chicago
politics

Web.

*history does repeat
it self...*

I wish to dedicate this work to my Grandchildren,
Web Leslie III, Finn Leslie, Nicole, DJ, Kemi,
Erick Gadaleta, Jack and Grant Aguirre, Will Leslie
in the interest that they might become even more
aware of the importance of learning history for the
lessons it teaches us allowing for a better and
more fulfilled life.

Acknowledgment VII

If it hadn't been for Corey Meade this collection of writings might never have been printed as he was responsible, not only for the design of this book, but for coaching me through the digital maze which so confuses we of the "older generation"! It was also due to his encouragement that this book has been published as it had been my plan to merely reproduce in minimal print for giving to my family. Thanks also has to go to Joanne, my wife, for her patience and always intelligent assistance in critique.

Prologue

1979

Contents x

Contents XI

NOW & THEN

There once was a sage who said that if we don't become students of history we will be destined to reliving it. Well it would seem that this was sound thinking!

Starting in the early 70's I took up the hobby of writing poems relating to current events.

Recently I came upon a selection of these writings which I had put away to be forgotten and in re-reading realized how often they closely related to today's world. While many covered events in Chicago and the state of Illinois, still a fair number were concerned with national and international happenings as well.

It seemed particularly fitting that this be revisited at this time since here we are in an important election year and much of the material covered in these poems had to do with the political events of the late 70's and 80's including a very interesting race pitting Jimmy Carter against Ronald Reagan.

What I found in this perusal was a little disturbing as well as somewhat encouraging in some cases. In review, we find that in 1979, all of 30 years ago, the Congress was tied up in debates on how to resolve the problems of making this country energy independent!! Sadat and Begin had met with Jimmy Carter at Camp David hammering out agreements including restriction of Israeli settlers building on the West Bank and Gaza. Stories about the financial difficulties of the 80's, 1987 crash to be specific, and congress's hunt to find the "culprits".

I mention being disturbed as it would appear that little was accomplished over these last 30 years in the solving of many of the serious problems and encouraging that we can still smile at this realizing that we lived through the turmoil of the past and so should be able to again.

As of this writing we are still very dependent on Middle Eastern oil. The only thing to come out of our energy concerns of the late 70's was the President's order that we should all adhere to a 55 MPH speed limit and we added a new level of bureaucracy with the Department of Energy which costs the tax payer over 1 billion dollars a year to function.

1978

SIMPLE

If each man were to concern himself
with his fellow man's rights
He need not be concerned for his own

WL 1/4/78

NEW POPE

Those cardinals in Rome sure changed their gears
They've been electing Italians as
popes for over 400 years
But now the Man to lead the churches soul
Is young Pope Paul II
Believe it or not... a Pole

WL 1/5/78

5

A WILL

Cause of Uncle Sam and his income tax
About making a will you can't relax

Before that trip to the pearly gate
You must take care of child and mate

Now one would think that it would be easy to say
How you'd like to give your money away

But in these days to draw up a will
Can get one a whopping legal bill

WL 4/1/78

COMMIE IN FRANCE

In my heart I feel a pang
For Valerie Gisgard D'Estange
That he has had to get in bed
With members of Le Party Red

WL 4/2/78

*A time when France was turning Communistic
and the then French Premier was required
to assemble a government including the
Red Party as a major power.*

HIGH TAX

Breaths there a tax payer with soul so dead
Who never to himself hath said
I don't think it's the least bit funny
The way you guys spend all my money

WL 4/3/78

SOCIAL SECURITY

The Social Security Act
Is broke and that's a fact

It was to keep us alive
After age sixty-five

A promise it may have to retract

WL 4/3/78

*In the news in April of 1978
we were told that the funding
was running out yet 30 years
later it's still paying as planned?*

SPEED JINGLE

There once was a driver named Cass
Who every car on the highway would pass

He said "Oh what fun"
"My engine to gun"

"Who cares how I'm wasting the gas"

WL 4/4/78

WATERGATE

This we hope will be the last Watergate act
The memoirs of Richard Nixon

The question arises – How much of it is fact
And just how much is fiction ?

WL 4/5/78

11

TAX JINGLE

There once was a taxpayer named Fred
Who to his congressman said

I don't think that it's funny
The way you took all my money

And still have a balance that is red

WL 4/19/78

WELL MAYBE

Ted Kennedy maintains that he won't run
That he has no desire to be number one

But I think it might be better if he would refrain
From appearing to always to be on campaign

WL 4/28/78

REALLY WANT PEACE?

Today our senate lunched with Mosha Dayan
Who pleaded "give us all the planes that you can
keep us strong and the Arabs weak
and you'll achieve the peace that we all seek"
But Carter thinks it only fair
To give both jets to fill the air
Don't you think the world would be better served
If the sale of arms would be somehow curbed?

WL 4/28/78

ERLICHMAN

Well John Erlichman is out of prison
And total freedom is now his'n
He says he'll write a book and state
All the details of Watergate
Will the day ever come do you suppose
When this chapter in our history will ever close?

WL 4/29/78

15

REPAIRS

I don't look forward to summer
Due to obstacles with which I contend

Driving the Tri-State is always a bummer
Thanks to construction around every bend

You'd think every project completed
They tear it up every doggone year

Ideas for busy work depleted
But this summer they'll find more I fear

WL 5/6/78

O'HARE AIRPORT

Someday I'd like to fly from O'Hare
And not have all the strain

Of trying to get through the repairs out there
And be on time for my plane

WL 5/7/79

17

RED BRIGADE

Moro is dead by the hand of the Red Brigade
For over a month they carried on their gruesome
charade

Giving Italy ample time to re*flect*
If the Reds gained power what to expect

It's pathetic to see in this vignette of strife
what little regard they have for human life

They've now taught the world that no difference exists
between they and all the other unscrupulous fascists

They are aptly named Reds for the blood that they spill
The innocent people that they maim and they kill

They've damaged their cause no question remains
What a shame for the suffering and many blood stains

WL 6/20/78

The Red Brigade, a terrorist group
operating in Italy, kidnapped the premier
and finally assassinate him.

18

JULY 4TH

Come the holiday 4th of July
It's a good idea to sit and think why

We're as lucky as any people can be
To live in this beautiful country

Sure! Many say that we don't have perfection
But we're sure headed in the right direction!

WL 7/5/78

19

PROGRESS

Consider the very goals we set
Are likely to change before they're met

Doesn't it seem incongruous to you
The statement "change is nothing new!"

Who was the genius that once said
When changes stop the man is dead

The reasonable man adapts himself
The unreasonable man will not

It's thanks to the unreasonable one
The world it's progress got

The trouble with our times you see
May be that the future is not what it used to be?

WL 7/21/78

GAS

Congress is holding up the entire nation
Whilst it argues about energy legislation

They threaten a filibuster so deregulation won't pass'
Now that's what I call "natural gas"!

WL 8/4/78

*Thirty years later (2008) and
we are still nowhere with energy.*

21

POSTAGE IS GOING UP

From the days our mail was pony expressed
Over the wild and treacherous trails of the west

To today when the carriers fight the cold and the heat
And brave dogs large and small nipping at their feet

We've been able to live in symphony
Feeling for them great empathy

But the time has come for we citizens to say
Seriously guys how much more can we pay?

WL 8/21/78

CAMP DAVID TALKS

"I'll do this if you do that"
Prime Minister Begin said to Sedat
Anwar said the Middle East will have peace
If settling the West Bank you will cease
The question is how far will they go
Without cooperation from the PLO
Who weren't included and were very sore
A feeling that was shared by our own press corp

WL 9/19/78

As it turned out they didn't go very
far as the problem still exists in 2008.

NOVEMBER SNOWFALL

It floats in soundlessly on padded feet
So unlike it's summer cousin
Purifying man's injustices to Mother Nature
And decorates denuded forms with sparkling white wrap
Whirling and dancing it both
delights and dismays simultaneously
It sings soft songs and chatters at the step in icy weather
Commanding by astounding numbers
gives up and goes as quietly
as it came
when touched by the warm spring
sun that will be here too soon

WL 11/6/78

NOVEMBER DREAM

A kaleidoscope of color
Gold embroidery in the evening sky
Bright colors wafting on the wind
Green struggling against brown
A gauzy morning mist
Flying creatures gather on wires to talk things over
Pungent odors of wood and pies
When the wind stops whispering and begins to shout
Black eyed Susan's wave goodbye
An occasional whiff of camphor
When the landscape stops looking painted and becomes
etched

WL 11/10/78

DIRTY POLITICS

It sounds like President Balaguer
Ain't playing the game completely square

He's stuffed the ballots his opponents swore
Down in the city of San Salvadore

But he says it's OK to do this you see
As it's all in the interest of democracy

WL 11/13/78

ZAIRE

You say to yourself why should we care
About the little country known as Zaire?

Well the Russians do
And the Cubans too

What they want for the communist hopper
Is all that valuable Kolwasi copper

And their intentions are not to be the least bit fair
To those poor human beings living there

WL 12/2/78

*Scare about communist
expansionism for strategic materials.*

TAIWAN

So long Taiwan it was so nice to know ya!
We're leaving your side but don't let it throw ya!

We've decided it would be more fun to swing
With those commies under Deng Hsaio Ping.

WL 12/18/78

*It was in this year of 78 that the US
made the diplomatic decision to abort
our agreement to acknowledge Taiwan's
independence from China.*

28

1979

ENDANGERED SPECIES

It crawls, it walks, it breaths in air
It takes just a reasonable amount of care

It lives on the earth with ever greater facility
Due to it's ever increasing agility

It invents all sorts of ingenious things
It's own light, heat, automation, even wings

It reads, it writes, it sings pretty songs
It develops rewards and punishments for rights and wrongs

It sometimes communicates with it's own kind
But also at times seems completely blind

To the wants and needs of others

In it's brilliance it has developed a terrible thing
That to this world total destruction could bring

A substance so hideous that in the event of strife
It could actually extinguish all the earth's life

This thing that must be controlled before it's too late
Is something man alone developed and it is called
HATE!

WL 2/3/79

MICHAEL AND THE SNOW FALL

Mayor Michael (Bilandic) has admitted to making mistakes
While Chicagoans are watching the snow as it cakes

But his major error, as his nose, is quite plain
It was giving a quarter million to his old crony Ken Sane

You can expect to hear a word or two from Calamity Jane
About the shenanigans tween' Mike and Ken Sane

If anymore graft the papers do discern
Young Michaels political hopes may "Byrne"

WL 2/25/79

Chicago had the snow storm of the century and Mayor Bilandic,
after taking the helm as Mayor Richard Daley had died,
was caught for giving a no bid snow plowing contract
to an old friend who couldn't perform and he was about
to enter into contest for the election for mayor with
a tough political opponent Jane Byrne. Byrne did finally
win this contest and the winter "mistake" was
a major reason for the Bilandic loss!

WINTER OF 79

Enough.. no more... I sit here and muse
Guess you could call it the old winter blues

I know once again I'm sure to be fine
If we ever see the spring of 79

WL 2/25/79

*1979 we had one of the worst
winters in Chicago history.*

SPRING OF 79

The world is filled with life again as our
air born friends return
Mother Nature's wrap is worn and marked to
be shed for leaf and fern

Man's transgressions become uncovered and
all too apparent for which we're all to blame
But bless her soul that grand old lady
will overcome and cover green our shame

WL 3/19/79

MIDEAST PEACE

The Egyptians, as always, say this and Sedat
While, as usual, Menachem is Begin

It looks like peace we'll finally see
Between Sedat the Egyptian and Begin the Israeli

The time has come in the Middle East
To emasculate that warlike beast

WL 3/24/79

The world thought that this was
finally it after a most encouraging meeting
at Camp David with the US President.

CHICAGO REPUBLICANS

Poor Wally Johnson by his party
has been spurned

And a good chance at the poles that
he will be "Byrned"

WL 3/25/79

*The republican party has never
been much of a factor in Chicago
but this was never more apparent
than in this election for mayor.
The party never even attempted to
get behind it's chosen candidate.*

ENERGY

I can't help thinking as I strive
To keep my speed at 55

The President struck a sensitive nerve
When he told those people who for him serve

Your parking space is no longer free
Like average citizens you must be

But will this rule he last night made
Appreciably our energy problem aid

He told the oil companies it will be fair
To charge for their product all the traffic will bare

And any increased profit they might make
From them in taxes he will take

Well if such a law the congress does pass
We're going to be paying a lot more for gas!

WL 4/6/79

*Interesting that in 79 we were in an
energy crunch and too beholden to foreign
oil and the President realized that this was
the case and proposed that we conserve and
one of the ways was to drive slower, thus the 55
speed limit, and he suggested that congress
pass a law that the oil companies could charge
as much as they "needed" for their product
and any "windfall" profit would be taxed. Well,
in hindsight, this may have been a bitter pill but
should have adopted as we would have changed
our ways, to some degree anyway, and thus maybe
have avoided the mess were in today! Instead 30
years has passed and now we are sending 700 billion
dollars out of the country to foreign countries
which is causing us a terrible trade deficit.* 38

FINALLY SPRING

Spring will be a little late this year
Or so the saying goes

As every day that rolls around
it either rains or snows

We, in Chicago, have this fright
That Chicken Little might be right!

WL 5/3/79

VERY LATE SPRING

Spring will be a little late this year
so goes the old refrain

and if it gets much colder my dear
we'll be getting snow instead of rain

I met a robin the other day
sounds odd I know but true

who said this must be December not May
my breast is not red it's blue

WL 5/8/79

MARGARET

The Labor Party couldn't match her
This iron lady named Margaret Thatcher

So now there comes upon the scene
Another British reigning queen

WL 5/10/79

*Briton's first lady prime minister
would go on to serve a long time and
she really led the way for the feminine
"revolution" of modern times.*

FALLING MARKET

Oh the days like this when the market is down
It causes poor investors like me to frown

And when you consider what a game of chance
This method used to your estate enhance

When the only thing that seems to rally
Are the gambling stocks like Ceasar's World and Bally

WL 5/14/79

*Here we have the stock market falling
just as we see it 30 years later and high
energy costs were complicit. The two
gambling stocks were the only ones to
rise this day!*

GARBAGE DAY

It's early Monday in the AM
and I hear those thunderous sounds
the banging, crashing, mayhem
as the collector makes his rounds

the noise at our curb
is simply absurd

somewhere out there I know there must
live the luckiest of man
they don't get around till noon to
empty his garbage can

WL 6/15/79

WRITE A BOOK

Remember when they used to say
that crime was something that didn't pay

Well now the thing is to become a crook
Then make a fortune writing a book

WL 6/20/79

*Principles from Watergate writing
books after serving prison terms.*

MARINAR FINDINGS

Thank the good Lord it is a relief to know
More about old planet Pluto
Here we thought that young Plutonians couldn't spoon
Due to not having any moon

But now we have found they DO!

WL 7/8/79

the space shot Marinar in
July of 78 found a hidden moon

LET EM! FIGHT IT OUT

It's too bad Komeni and the Shah of Iran
Couldn't square off man to man

Instead of causing the suffering of so many souls
On the way to accomplishing their own selfish goals

WL 7/19/79

IRISH WASTE

A young girl got in the way
Of the wild and irresponsible work of the IRA
And died!

Lord Mountbatten did fall
To the bottom of the bay of Donegal

These were tragic things and they say
Both events were the work of the IRA

Such a terrible waste of human life
What will this do for Northern Ireland's strife?

The foundation of freedom is severely shaken
Each time a life is needlessly taken

And so we say to the IRA
For humanity's sake put your guns away

There are better ways to achieve your desire
Without setting your beautiful green world on fire

WL 8/12/79

A POLITICAL YEAR

There is reason to believe from what we hear
that 1980 will become known as THE political year

the presidential race is shaping up to be
the political event of the century

the Republican Party seems without a head
and if this keeps up it might just be dead

Dole says he's not an organizational man
though he belongs to the party Republican

Reagan has not yet begun his push
If not soon there may not be a bird in the hand
rather one in a BUSH

Is it possible where the office once had a Quaker
That the day might come when it is filled by a Baker

or could we hear a fireside homily
delivered by an ex-democrat Connally

and all these men had better be ready
to take on the new conservative Teddy

though the electorate might feel it is going too far
choosing yet another guy who changes a's to r.

and turn to another democratic family of renown
by electing the liberal Californian Brown

still we have to consider that tortoise like starter
the quiet,tenacious,incumbent Carter

so far those mentioned seem certainly to be
the most formidable ships on our political sea

yet a another voice is heard from the Mid-Western plain
the resonant sound of ultra-conservative Crane

though more contestants in the race may seem a plague
we must not fail to mention Gen. Alexander Haig

a fair passel I'd say this group that we mention
these intelligent men in bitter contention

what fascination in this office that these men can see
escapes any understandable logic to me

the one who snatches this questionable jewel
gets a chance a recalcitrant party to rule

may also reap the rewards gained by President Jim (Carter)
and from out here that reward looks pretty grim
How would you like it if it were you

who had to fight for the signing of the treaty Salt ll
or sit and watch your reputation spoil

as the result of excessive profits made
from the high price of oil

and there certainly can't be any real delight
in failing to solve Cambodia's plight

and what pleasure can there be in curing inflation
by increasing unemployment in our nation

to be so frustrated in getting Iran to agree
that the decent thing to do is the hostages free

be the object of so much media derision
each time you make a foreign policy decision

the issues to face the winner in 80
promise to be even more weighty

49

No! it's no bowl of cherries this position of president
watch the tube, read the papers, it becomes quite evident

yet so many willingly donate political blood
and stand there exposed to the slinging of mud

what makes these men want to work so hard
to hoist themselves on there own political petard

I guess that it doesn't pay to be so analytical
when investigating the mind of the animal political

it seems to make one encourage his daughter or son
to become a doctor,lawyer or fireman

well,let's hope that the victory is very decisive
and the campaign rhetoric not quite so derisive

WL 11/4/79

1980

DIFFERENT BUT ALIKE

How many of us are there?
Too numerous to count?
Some say 3 1/2 billion and
every second the figures mount.

All homosapien, we share that silly name
But in that name only are we the same

Isn't it amazing how different we all can be
Never two of the same sets of fingerprints will
we ever see

Dentures / eyes / follicles of hair
None of these things do any of us share

Yet as different as we are
We would all agree by far

There is something we do share
Two needs about which we do care

LOVE and RESPECT

WL 1/1/80

REAGAN AND THE CONTRA

Washington DC is not the place
The fox is likely to win the race

Twist and turn as quick as he can
There's just no shaking that deal with Iran

The air is filled with the excited sounds
Of the pack of investigating blood thirsty hounds

Another direction he'd better go forth
As he is in deep trouble for turning to NORTH

WL 1/3/80

*President Reagan Had Oliver North
testify at Contra Hearings in his behalf.*

ISLAM DISTORTED

Tell me Ayatollah if you can
What's this religion you have in Iran

Which has shown the world ever new heights
in the removing any semblance of human rights

Your latest move has helped the world to see
Just how despotic a ruler can be

It would seem that you've done about all that you can
To discourage belief in your religion Islam

WL 1/4/80

SHOULD WE?

Here we let the Iranian students roam
When maybe we ought to send them home

So they could be there first hand to see
what a just and decent ruler the Ayatollah can be

View how he has gone to ever new heights
In removing any semblance of human rights

WL 1/5/80

*Question in Congress about deporting Iranian students
attending college in the U.S. While American hostages
are held in Iran.*

ECCENTRIC

Envy he who lives with his own world
Suffer the wounds of non-compliance
He, at least, remains as a pillar of granite
Admired finally by generations well removed

Pity conversely the conformist who has no world
Who changes with the hours and
becomes like them unremembered
And while passing through feels little warmth

WL 1/6/80

NEW PRESIDENT?

Well the battle is not over it is plain to see
There is still a chance for Bush and Ted Kennedy

The verbiage goes on and the debate grows quite hot
Contestants not saying what they are... rather what their
opponent is not!

What I'm afraid they may prove when it is over and done
Is... a man qualified to be president.. among them there is
none!

WL 4/23/80

ED MUSKIE

For our new Secretary of State President Jimmy said
The best I believe I can find is Senator Ed

No known genius in foreign affairs is he
But certainly a sop to the Congress he'll be

It remains to be seen Mr. President Sir!
Whether or not you have a Muskie that is
out of his water

WL 5/2/80

CHICAGO SCHOOL BUSING

The Chicago school budget must be reduced we say
No more extra attendants on the bus

Can't you find another way
Parents cry "don't put the burden on us"

About their kids behavior these parents should show
some concern
The money saved from extra busing costs could help their
children learn

WL 9/4/80

*Due to serious misbehavior of
students being bussed the city had
added security personnel and were planning
to remove same and parents were
bitterly complaining.*

61

POLES ARE FREE

The Russian bear is having a fit
Now that the light of freedom in Poland is lit

The tune of freedom is not
played from the Baltic to Murmansk
But no matter... The polish workers are going to Gdansk

WL 9/7/80

The Poles are the first communist group
to opt for freedom when Leck Lawensa
organized at Gdansk shipyards.

LOVE

It defies all our senses five
This elusive thing
It keeps our very hearts alive
And makes our libidos sing

It has great value yet can't be bought
It is the precious ingredient from
Which peace is wrought

He who won't give it but expects to receive
Will find he badly does himself deceive

An emotional well must be dug
Using the tool of giving
That the void be filled with love
Is the real secret of living

WL 9/17/80

COMING ELECTION

Tuesday is the day we give offices away
The day the electorate will probably say

Tho you tried very hard things weren't quite right
You've asked us too often the bullet to bite

So someone new will take your office I fear
To see if they can put the economy in gear

Me! I'll never be a politician unless maybe
I could kiss the mothers and...
shake hands with the baby

WL 11/14/80

1981

THE COMMUTER

The pensive faces
All in their places

Being carted off to doom?
Can it be that bad?
That they look so sad
Smile... Enough of this gloom

Very sturdy souls are we
Who stand and wait for the 8:03

The wind blows it's ice cold breeze
The kind that chills through the bvd's

We crowd like cattle in a group
Pondering our actions while in the loop

Only to return on the 5:41
Exhausted from the work we've done

WL 4/20/81

Ever look at the faces staring
out of commuter train windows?

A NEW SEASON

Delicate, fresh green, etched with deep, rich black lines

The honking of a leader showing
His charges the way home from vacation

Incessant chatter from a cast of thousands
Who won't let the dawn sneak up on you
But excitedly speak of the warmth to come

A washed smell to excite the imagination
Of things to come

The world noisily stretches, yawns and
Prepares for a new day.

We have gently laid winter to rest

WL 5/3/81

ANOTHER NEW SEASON

It's that vibrant time of year
When the earth yawns and stretches
Bright blades of grass poke their heads up looking
for things to do
Daffodils nod to them
Sometimes shuddering in the chill breeze
The cardinal loudly announces that
this is his territory
Having lots of competition at the first light of day

WL 5/6/80

POPE SHOT

This insanity has gone too far
One wonders where the boundaries are

Another Man we know got holes
Walking this earth saving souls

WL 5/11/81

HUNGER STRIKE

A tragedy the souls on fire
These Ulster men of wild desire

We stand and watch as day by day
They intentionally drain their lives away

What good do you suppose they will reap
By making human life seem so cheap

WL 5/22/81

*Northern Irish dissidents held
by the British die on hunger strike.*

CTA CRISIS

The poor commuters watch the politicians play
Janey says she is taking over the CTA

"But never you mind. Just sit back and relax
We're merely reducing service and adding a 4% tax

The riders don't think it very funny
Her trying to make them believe
someone else will pay
that money

WL 6/11/81

Jane Byrne, the mayor, took
over the running of the CTA.

1984

TOYS IN THE ATTIC

Some nerve gas we have got has become obsolete
We've found more inventive ways the enemy to defeat

Now the problem that is really tough
How do we dispose of the hideous stuff?

God forbid we have some fanatic
Start playing around with those toys in the attic

WL 2/18/84

*In 84 we found a forgotten
inventory of lethal gas to be disposed of.*

THE ELUSIVE SEASON

Where did it go?
A feeling lonesome... homesick... no!
Nostalgic is a better word
The choc-choc of the lobster boat and
fresh, sweet blueberries
The world coming alive at 5 AM in a slight haze
Buzzing things in the late afternoon
Green upon green upon green
The nocturnal squeal of tires and a dog barking
off in the distance
The cry of the Blue jay
A cottage with the smell of wood and kerosene
Laughter over the water and splashing
Ice cold beer and the crack of a bat
Or tart drinks and the clop of a tennis ball
A trickle of sweat and sensuous shade
Fragrance of just cut grass
The tug on the line... is it a weed just playing tricks?
Birds in symphony announcing the sun
The loon on the lake... a spot of mustard
Bees / bugs / buzzing mosquitoes /ice cream / hot dogs /
mint / crickets and ants / fresh, cold melon

The world is napping but it's beginning
to stretch and wake up
Getting ready for the run and "it's"
here before you know it.
Oh Oh! There's dew on the lawn

It was all here but it went so quickly
Please bring it back because I missed some!
Oh! Never mind. Toss me the ball and go out for a pass

WL 8/18/84

1987

OCTOBER 1987

Black Monday a day we should never forget
The day that reality and the stock market met

When so many were rolling in mythical cash
And that fickle hearted market decided to crash

Now the experts are locked in the fascinating game
Of trying to find a culprit to name

Some point to the computer saying " there is our Fagen"
While others say it's obviously President Reagan

Some say the falling dollar you cannot excuse
Or could it be the trouble in the Straits of Hormuz?

The latest cry is it's deficit spending
On which the market's health is depending

Come on! fellas let's get serious
Is the investment community downright delirious?

Once upon a time a company's financial wealth
was directly related to it's security's health

You put money in a company for investment sake
Not to help some raider the Board Chairman to break

Let's go back to the time when a stock's value was real
Not filled full of air for an Ichan deal

Wall Street better stop the pyramidal trading
Investors confidence is seriously fading

And if they don't start getting some solidity there
One day they'll open the cage
and find neither a bull nor a bear

WL 10/19/87

*It is now 2008, exactly 21 years later and we
have the same problem and the experts are trying
to assess blame for this latest market crash!*

IN THOSE HEADY DAYS OF 1987

Frivolity was a friend to all or at least so it seemed.
Until, one day, Reality came along with
her ugly face and harsh manners.
She kicked and screamed and bit a few.

Strange, though, how she turned out
to be the most trustworthy one

WL 10/21/87

*"Reality" proved herself
again in October 2008.*

1991

JUSTICE CLARENCE

When the final star is extinguished
And our planet is lit for day
For insight to honesty we pray

A man and woman of color
Each articulate and smart
Are telling us a story
But their versions are worlds apart

If hers is true the man is a monster
behind the perfect mask
But if it's true, what she states, why hasn't his
cover dropped before this we ask?

No matter how disgusting the story.
Terrible and uncouth.
Before we find him guilty, remember,
we must see some actual proof!

WL 10/11/91

The Senate confirmation hearings
for Surpreme Court Justice Clarence Thomas,
who was finally confirmed.

1994

SARAJEVO SHELLED

Serb gunners are unconscionable brutes
They will kill at the drop of a hat

They will lie and cheat to achieve their end
you can bet an Englishmen's life on that

Death dealing explosives rained out of the skies
As they said that the color of white they didn't recognize

WL 7/27/94

Written commemorating the shelling
of a peace march in Sarajevo when an
Englishman was killed and the
Serb Army gunners denied seeing
a white flag leading the marchers.

MORALS

We may be entering into an amoral night
Where two wrongs do make a right!

WL 9/4/1994

20
01

SEPTEMBER 11

Terrible that there should be so much bad in this world
But then that is how good is really understood

Man has many foibles not the least of which is
despair

So it must be remembered that foul weather is always
followed by
fair

Should your day be touched with sorrow
remember...
If He thought it perfect He would not have invented
tomorrow

WL 10/29/01
Revised 8/11/07

ON THE SHELF

I feel this need to be needed
A sad and silly quirk

That has been bothering me
Ever since my quitting work

I'm occupied with serious decisions now
Will it be golf, tennis, or going for a swim

Looking down the front of me I realize
I should be running to the gym

I meet all these nice people
While on my morning walks

Oh yes! They'll often nod or smile
But no one ever talks

I used to pray for good weather
For when I waited for the train

Now I get so much sunshine
I find myself praying for some rain

There must be something for which I'm needed
But until that thing is found

I think I'll just saunter over to the golf course
And play another round

WL 11/15 /O1

93

20
02

COULD BE WORSE

Being in difficulty is a not a fun place to be
But not so bad if even some hard solutions you see

Remember...

It's a better place - by far!
Than being lost and not knowing where you are!

WL 7/29/02

2004

NOVEMBER 11

Today I looked into the setting sun
Thinking of all my wars you've won

It's overwhelming to think you gave your whole life for me
Just so I might live and love and each day be free

I don't know how much you suffered
were you hot? were you cold?
Did you experience a great deal of pain?

Today I say a prayer for you... but you
know that it's sad and a shame
Because with all you've done for me
I don't even know your name!

WL 11/11/04

20
06

HEALTHY/WEALTHY AND WISE?

We spend a monumental amount of time
at considerable cost to our
health
Accumulating glitzy things, trinkets
the material markers of
wealth
Then in these later years seems odd but true
we spend so much of what we have left of that
wealth
In a feverish, frenzied spending spree
to see if we can't protect or recover our
health

WL 6/7/06

20
07

OLD

We humans have a rather morbid
fascination with age

man in his genius invented the
measurement of "year"

parties to celebrate our antiquity
are all the rage

but we certainly miss the point I fear

what's more important... what you have done? or merely
the calculation of... how long you have run?

WL 3/9/07

PRESIDENT

What should the qualifications be for winning this race
Well let's hope it is more than Hillary's smiling face

Newt seems to feel that one can win the game
Having achieved, what is a rather dubious fame

Or let's take John who thinks it makes no difference
that he lost before
"I'll win by merely railing against the war"

Then we have Rudy who thinks the job he can master
Based on his handling of one terrible disaster

The anti war group would go insane
Should we elect John McCain

We better be very careful about the integrity of the one
we get to fill this space
Lest we end up, worse than now, being between
Iraq and a hard place!!

WL 3/11/07

A YEAR

Who says a year is really a year?
Someone's been tampering with the calendar I fear

Years used to be much much longer
Back when I was younger and stronger

What happened last Monday is a complete haze
Now doesn't that prove that we have been skipping some
days?

There's something wrong I'll tell you and here's a clear sign
Days have started going bye two at a time!

When, on Saturday, you can't even remember there
being a Thursday well it becomes abundantly clear
That a year is really no longer a year

I was asked...
"What did you do last Sunday son?"
I had to answer...
"Sorry sir but we didn't have one"!

Now don't you think that it is rather queer
That we now have only 25 weeks in a year?

WI 4/4/07

20
08

REFUGEE

It starts with a vulgar amount of greed
the kind on which fanatics feed

the objective is grab all you can
to hell with how it affects your fellow man

first comes words, then destruction and killing
it's easy to find simple minded killers willing

then the sad pictures of tents and tear stained faces
humans condemned to living in awful places

families whose lives will never be the same
proud peoples sentenced to living in unwarranted shame

This could be the story of you or me
it is the sad saga of the refugee

WL 4/3/08

DEAR CITY HALL

I went shopping for groceries the other day
And was amazed at how unconscionably your taking
our money away

Looking at the final bill to see where it went
Saw the shocking figure at the bottom of TAX 10%

I'm afraid Todd Stroger has flipped his wig
If he thinks that we can live with a tax that big

And as though that weren't enough
There was an added 3% more tax for other stuff

Told some of that 3% was a tax on "sin"
Guess that last three depends on whose pew your in

Please let me know the next time you and the aldermen
vote for tax on sin
The discussion by that group should be fascinating and
I'd like to sit in

And you know driving from Cook County to Lake
ain't going too far
When you realize that you could save a couple thousand
when buying a car

My advice sir for all you at City Hall
You may be riding for an electoral fall

In November when the voting booths are empty
the voters might just be
Down at the Chicago River's edge dumping
in cases of "Tea"

WL 8/16/08

SOCIALISM

It's proven every day
Handing someone something
More oft-times takes away

WL 8/18/08

SOME THOUGHTS

Man doesn't realize how hideous
war is until he is killed... and then it's too late!

Don't be guided by events, rather make them!

May you live as long as you wish
and wish to as long as you live.

He knows more than he understands

Beware of one man bands as they soon run out of tunes

I have no claim to financial fame
and it doesn't bother me greatly

And now that the market is the way it is
there are many more joining me lately

COME ON! ONE MORE DRINK I INSIST
AND TOMORROW BECOMES YESTERDAY...
THAT YOU MISSED!

WL 8/20/08

IS THERE TIME?

Another time another place
Another man with younger face

He's still there that man I knew
With still many more things to do

Is there time ?
Well don't waste it!

WL 10/1/08

CUBS OF 08

Oh! It hurts... it hurts sooo much
There are some subjects too sensitive to touch
It was sooo much fun
To watch the hit and the run
But then the team had to lose in the clutch

WL 10/5/08

THE CANDIDATE

He murmured "apple pie"
You might even hear "mother" as a sigh

A platform of platitudes?

A rule.. Don't disturb the delicate tissue
by making a definite comment on any issue

Isn't a shame that we can't see
What the candidate, in action, might really be

But the fabric changes like the seasons
An attitude can switch for so many reasons

So how do we accurately rate this woman or man
Well search out their soul... if you can

How do they live from day to day
This is far more telling than what they say

Look to their actions do they compare with their "truth"
And don't be mislead by age nor impressed by youth

What reactions when they're in a struggle
A straight forward move or do they tend to juggle

In which camp do they comfortably live
Is it that of Liberal, Independent, or is it Conservative?

However be careful not to judge by the name
But see if actions are befitting the same

To the office they aspire, what is the lure?
Can you be sure that their intentions are pure?

Wouldn't it be nice if we could resort
To a complete analysis
giving profile with psychological report

But alas and alack we must realize at last
That the only way to really judge is to look at their past

Go back as far as you can – if possible all the way
Do they have a record of living up to what they say

Don't be satisfied with a report from yesterday

WL 10/5/08

SECRETARYS OF STATE

Last night Condoleezza played piano for the Queen
Saying that this may be the last time she'll be seen

Queen Elizabeth thought the performance quite nice
And said she would miss our Secretary of State Rice

And we only wish, your Highness, we could say
We knew what kinds of tunes her replacement will play

WL 12/2/08

POOR JOHN

Many feel sorry for John McCain's presidential bid fail'in

But he has himself to blame for picking
his running mate Palin

WL 12/5/08

MADE OFF WITH THE CASH

The name is Bernie Madoff. That's pronounced (made-off) if you please
Guess I'll be known, for a long time to come, as the king of financial sleaze

But you know these last few years I haven't been alone in what I've done
You have to realize with the failures on Wall Street that I'm not the only one

There have been some real experts working on this street
Some really brilliant characters I think the Feds should like to meet

Am afraid the truth is our society got a bit too greedy
And so now we have become a nation populated with an over supply of
needy

If we ever get through the fallout from this most recent busted bubble
Let's all try to be more diligent in watching out for trouble

My Dad once said "Son when investing money you should know
that all things that come too easy, just as easy go!"

As history remembers Ponzi's fame
and refers to swindles using his name

So will from this day forth be a memory of
Bernard's house of cards

WL - 12/17/08

2009

DEAR JET BLUE

WHOA! WAIT A MINUTE.. THERE'S SOMETHING WRONG HERE
YOUR RULES ARE VERY INEQUITABLE I FEAR

HATE TO BE THE ONE TO MAKE A FUSS
BUT YOU KEEP TELLING ME "YOUR VERY IMPORTANT TO US"

WEEKS IN ADVANCE AND FOR GOOD REASON
I MUST CHANGE MY FLIGHT
AND TO DO THIS YOU CHARGE ME $75.00!
DO I HAVE THAT RIGHT?

YET YOU CANCEL MY FLIGHT FOR

LACK OF A CREW
(AND OFTEN AT THE LAST MINUTE)
BUT YOU TELL ME "NO WAY CAN I CHARGE YOU"!

YOU CHARGE ME.....WRONG
I CAN'T CHARGE YOU....WRONG

DEAR JET BLUE DO YOU SEE MY PLIGHT?
ACCORDING TO MY LOGIC TWO WRONGS DO NOT MAKE A
RIGHT!!

WL - 1/8/09

128

WHERE HAVE ALL THE
STATESMEN GONE

When you look at Illinois politics isn't it sad
To see how some politicians can be so bad

You take Stratton,Kerner,Walker,Ryan
Out of the last seven govenors now there is Rod Blagojevich
they'll be try'n

When you listened to his phone conversations it was quite absurd
How he could find so many uses for that four letter word

The Committee to Impeach vote tallyed and only one vote against
but..there was a slight flaw
As that one vote was cast by his sister-in-law

When they get to high office there seems this overwhelming need
To find devious ways to satisfy their greed

What happened to the statesman who said
"I'll do all that I can
To improve this world for my fellow man"??

WL-1/31/09

I'M SICK

I felt pretty good when I got up but then I turned on TV
It was then that I learned just how sick I could be!

My eyes did burn a little bit and they were dry too
But I was told that my problem would be solved with just a drop of Clear-Vu.

Oh! and I'd better not forget to call the Doc
and get a prescription for that antacid that works around the clock

I was anxious to see something about the election
But had to wade through a serious warning regarding a four hour erection??

And the scene of two people holding hands, both in their own tubs
not inside the house but out.
Now what is that imagery all about??

"Oh! I can't sleep" she says with an exhausted sigh
and what is the drug company's solution?
They are going to send her a blue/green butterfly!

"Look out ,your blood is about to clot"
and it's all because of old Aunt Dot

"Not to worry about what you eat" "You have no control"
"It's not your fault"
It's all because of Uncle Walt!

Come on guys give me a break
A little less advertising for entertainment's sake

I am very sorry if I sound a bit sour
But I actually am getting sick... from watching 54 commercials per hout

W1-2/2/09

130

HILLARY

Hillary is on a trip to Jakarta and Beijing
And it would seem she is experimenting with an interesting thing

Just maybe international government negotiation we don't need as much
As showing the world a human touch

WL- 2/21/09

Made in the USA